SAVED

What is Salvation
and Why is it Necessary?

ROD NICHOLS

Publishing Coordinator – Sharon Kizziah-Holmes

Paperback-Press
an imprint of A & S Publishing
Paperback Press, LLC.
Springfield, Missouri

ISBN -13: 978-1-964559-47-6

ACKNOWLEDGMENTS

First, I want to acknowledge God for saving my life through the death of His Son, Jesus and for the new life I am now living, because of the resurrection of Christ.

Second, I want to thank my wife, Karen, for her patience with and encouragement for my writing.

I also want to thank my editor Jenn Bateman for her good work, Sharon Kizziah-Holmes at Paperback Press for her work in the professional layout of the book and Jaycee DeLorenzo for the amazing cover.

Thanks to Melani Pyke for the incredible cover art. You can find her art at melpyke.com.

TABLE OF CONTENTS

Acknowledgments

Introduction

Chapter One... 1

The Fall

Chapter Two 5

Expecting Jesus

Chapter Three 11

The Gift of Grace

Chapter Four... 15

God and Satan

Chapter Five 27

Hell and Heaven

Chapter Six... 33

The Proof is in the Fruit

Chapter Seven 37

What's Next

Author's Note... 42

About the Author.. 43

INTRODUCTION

I grew up in Denver, Colorado, and every Sunday my family went to the small denominational church across the street. I have to say that I hated it. In fact, many Sundays I would hide under the covers in my bed hoping they would forget me. They never did. The service was only an hour, but as a kid, that seemed like ten hours. We sat on hard wooden pews, listened to an off-key choir sing a couple of hymns, and then the minister droned on about something that was of no interest to me. Unfortunately, I never remember them talking about salvation – what it is or why it was necessary. So, at eighteen I left Denver to attend college in Tacoma, WA, and I was not saved. At that point in time, I made a commitment to never set foot in a church except for a wedding or funeral. I held solid to that commitment until I was forty.

It was during my fortieth year that I began to feel like there was something missing. Oh, I had accomplished a lot in my career already. We owned a big home, nice cars, and I was recognized as one of the best in my field. My marriage was fairly good. Our kids were doing okay. Yet, I felt empty. Many people talk about a God-shaped hole, and I sure had one. I tried filling it with career, money, prestige, alcohol, sports, sex, and travel, but nothing seemed to fill that hole. I was what is known as a seeker.

In during high school, oldest daughter started going to a church youth group with a friend. My wife would drop her off and pick her up every week. After a few months of that, she started going to weekly services and taking our kids. Having five kids, it was nice to have some peace and quiet for a few hours every week. Even though I saw them changing, I stuck firmly to my commitment of avoiding church.

In 1995, after watching my family become more fulfilled, peaceful, and joyful, I began thinking about giving church another try. One thing that attracted my attention was their comments about how great the music was there. Since I'm a product of the 60's and 70's, the greatest era for music, and my only reference for church music was the gray-haired lady playing the pipe organ, I just had to go and find out about the music. So, I told my wife that I'd like to join them for the Sunday night service. After I left the room, she went into our walk-in closet and did a happy dance. She had been praying for me.

That night, it was the music that captured my heart. Actually, it was the Holy Spirit, through the music. I was hooked and began attending every Sunday night. I was beginning to feel better about my life, but strangely, the God-shaped hole was still there. Then, one Sunday they announced that for the next week, there would be a dramatic performance of *Heaven's Gates and Hell's Flames* every night. We decided to go.

The night of the performance, we were running late

and ended up in the balcony. Shortly after we arrived, the lights went out and a spotlight hit the stage. A combination of professional actors and church members acted out short vignettes in which good people died and went to heaven. Jesus would open the book of life and if their name was there (meaning they had accepted Jesus as their Savior), He would escort them into heaven. If their name was not there, loud music would begin playing, strobe lights would pulse and two people dressed as demons would come and drag the person kicking and screaming off to hell. Now, I'm not the sharpest tack in the box, so it took three or four of these before it hit me. I could never be good enough to get into heaven, which meant that when I died, I was going to spend eternity in hell. I remember whispering that several times, "I'm going to hell." When they called people forward to receive Jesus as their Savior, I couldn't get down the steps fast enough. Well, truth be told, I was very careful on the steps down, as I didn't want to fall, break my neck, and die on my way down to get saved. I know now that the moment I recognized my need for Jesus as my personal savior, I was saved. More on that later.

After my salvation moment, I kept hearing that I was a new creation, but I didn't really feel any different than I did before. Oh, the God-shaped hole was now filled, but I was still thinking and doing the same things I did before I was saved. Finally, I learned that it was my spirit that was renewed, but my soul (mind, will, and emotions) had to be transformed to be aligned with my spirit. In other words, I had to become more like Jesus, my Savior.

Over the years since that time, I've planted and pastored two churches, traveled and taught in churches up and down the west coast, and served as an associate pastor at a few churches. I've also written and published several Christian books. Because of these experiences, I've encountered many people, yes even people going to church every Sunday, who don't understand salvation or why it's even necessary. I've explained it hundreds of times, which is why I'm writing this book. I want the same thing that Father God wants- that no one would perish. That everyone would enjoy eternal life in heaven.

If you don't understand salvation or why it's necessary or have friends or family who don't, this is the perfect book. It's short and easy to read. Literally, it will change your life and your eternal future, so read on, my friend!

CHAPTER ONE

THE FALL

To better understand salvation, we must go back to the beginning of humanity. In the beginning, God created the universe and the earth. He prepared the earth for occupation by man and then formed man out of the dust of the earth. God then breathed His Spirit into the man and gave him dominion over the earth. Realizing that Adam, the man, needed a companion, God formed woman, Eve, from one of his ribs and they were to rule together as equals. (Reference: Genesis 1 and 2)

God created a system that would provide everything that Adam and Eve needed to survive. He told them they could eat from any tree except the tree of the knowledge of good and evil. God intended Adam and Eve and all of mankind to live forever in paradise, but because they were disobedient and ate from the forbidden tree, they were cast out of paradise and into the world. Their disobedience was sin. God's holiness and sin cannot exist together. So, mankind and God were separated. (Reference: Genesis 3)

Unfortunately, this was not just a separation of Adam and Eve with God, rather it extended to all of humankind. Sin had impacted the DNA of the first humans and the physical death process began. Keep in mind that prior to the impact of sin, humans would have been immortal. However, sin brought eventual death into the picture. Adam lived 930 years. His son, Seth lived 912 years. Enosh lived 905 years. You can easily see the number of years declining. That said, there was one big exception, a man named Methuselah.

Methuselah lived to be 969 years. He lived longer than his father, Enoch, because God took Enoch to heaven alive when he was only 365 years old. Methuselah's extended life appears to have more to do with God's will than the natural progression of death due to sin. Methuselah was a form of prophecy. His name means "man of the sending forth." Church tradition says that it was at the time of Methuselah's birth that God revealed to Enoch that He was going to destroy the world the year Methuselah died, but that He would send forth a remnant man. We know that man to be Noah. The length of time between when Methuselah was born and when Noah entered the ark is 969 years.

After the great flood, the years of man's life began to drop dramatically. Noah's son, Shem lived 600 years. Further down the lineage, Abraham lived 175 years. His son Isaac lived 180 years. Jacob lived

147 years and Joseph lived 110 years. We know today that a person is a sort of rock star if they make it to 100 years and that's with all our modern medicine.

More importantly than the impact sin had on natural life, is the impact it had on spiritual life. In the Garden of Eden, God walked and talked with Adam and Eve prior to their moment of disobedience. However, that moment caused them to die spiritually, and they could no longer be in the presence of Holy God, or they would immediately die. God, out of love for His children, sent them out of the Garden of Eden, so they could no longer eat from the tree of life. As a loving Father, God didn't want His children to have to deal with the guilt and shame of their sin for all eternity. Plus, He had a plan for restoring His relationship with humanity.

Sacrifice

God's restoration plan was in two parts – both requiring sacrifice and blood. The first part was a system of animal sacrifice. I'm not going to spend a lot of time describing this, as it's very complicated and was hard even for the people of that time to understand. The essence of this system was that people could bring an animal that would be sacrificed for their sin. Blood must be spilled for sin to be covered. However, the blood of animals could never take away the sin or the accompanying guilt and shame (See Hebrews 10:4), so there needed to be a part two.

The issue is that legally the sacrifice of an animal could not eliminate or atone for the sin of a man. A perfect, sinless man would have to shed his blood and die, representing all of mankind, in order for the sin of all mankind to be atoned. The problem was that there weren't any perfect men or women on earth. So, the answer was for God to become a man, He had to be born as a human and live the typical human life. He must remain sinless and then die the sacrificial death to eliminate the power of sin for all mankind. Jesus was that man. He was God in flesh. Since the sinful nature was passed through the male, Jesus had to be born of God through the Holy Spirit and a virgin woman. So, unlike all other men, there was no sin in him at birth. All he had to do was remain sinless, even though he was tempted in every way, as all people are.

In the animal sacrificial system, it was a perfect, flawless lamb that was sacrificed for sin. Jesus was the perfect lamb of God, sacrificed for all the sin of all mankind. The key is blood. Animal sacrifice was part of the Old Testament Covenant, which required the shedding of animal blood to cover sin. Jesus, with his death on the cross, brought a new covenant, between God and man, initiated with the blood of Jesus. In the courts of heaven, the blood of Jesus speaks loudly for all humankind. More on that in the next chapter.

CHAPTER TWO

EXPECTING JESUS

Throughout the Old Testament in the Bible, we can find predictions or prophecies about this man, Jesus. Here are a few examples:

Isaiah 7:14, "Therefore the Lord himself will give you a sign: The virgin will conceive and give birth to a son and will call him Immanuel." Immanuel means God with us. So, this was a prophecy about God becoming a man and living with us. This occurred when a young virgin named Mary was overwhelmed by the Holy Spirit, gave birth to a son, and named him Yeshua, which is Hebrew for Jesus. This prophecy, written by Isaiah, was given over 700 years before Jesus' birth.

Micah 5:2, "But you Bethlehem Ephrathah, though you are small among the clans of Judah, out of you will come for me one who will be ruler over Israel, whose origins are from of old, from ancient times." This predicts the place of Jesus' birth, which is quite interesting, because his mother, Mary, lived in a town called Nazareth. However, Jesus wasn't born in Nazareth. A Roman census caused Mary and her husband, Joseph to travel to Bethlehem, where Jesus was born, fulfilling the prophecy that was given approximately 800 years before his birth.

Hosea 11:1, "When Israel was a child, I loved him, and out of Egypt I called my son." After Jesus was born in Bethlehem, Joseph was warned by an angel to take Jesus to Egypt, because the king was killing all the boys two years and younger, in an attempt to stop the birth of the Messiah/King of the Jews. After that king died, the angel returned to Joseph and told him it was safe to take Jesus back to Nazareth, where he grew up. This prophecy was also given about 800 years before the birth of Jesus.

Beyond Jesus' birth, there are also many prophecies about his death. Here are a few of those:

Psalm 22:16-18, "Dogs surround me, a pack of villains encircles me; they pierce my hands and my feet. All my bones are on display; people stare and gloat over me. They divide my clothes among them and cast lots for my garment." We see these fulfilled through the crucifixion of Jesus. According to Matthew 27:39 and Mark 15:29, they mocked and hurled insults shaking their heads at Jesus. They pierced his hands and feet during the crucifixion in Matthew 27:35. They divided his clothes and cast lots for his seamless robe in Matthew 27:35, Mark

15:24, and Luke 23:34. This prophecy was given by King David (a relative of Jesus) about 1000 years before the birth of Jesus. This is quite interesting because crucifixion didn't exist at the time of David. The first documented crucifixion was in 519 when King Darius of Persia crucified 3,000 of his political enemies in Babylon. Later it was perfected by the Romans and used as the method to kill Jesus. The accuracy of David's prophecy about Jesus' death is staggering.

Isaiah, 700 years before the birth of Jesus, also prophesied about his crucifixion in Isaiah 53:5, "But he was pierced for our transgressions, he was crushed for our iniquities; the punishment that brought us peace was on him, and by his wounds we are healed." Again, about 200 years before the invention of crucifixion, the prophet Isaiah sees the method of Jesus' death.

Jesus was from a lower-class family, so he would not have been buried with wealthy people, yet in Isaiah 53:9, it is prophesied that he would die with the wicked and be buried with the rich. "He was assigned a grave with the wicked, and with the rich in his death, though he had done no violence, nor was any deceit in his mouth." Jesus was crucified between two known criminals and then buried in the tomb of Joseph Arimathea, a very rich man. Also, Jesus wasn't crucified for crimes, and he had not conducted acts of violence, rather he was killed because of the envy of religious leaders. Another prophecy fulfilled.

The fact that these prophecies were so accurately

fulfilled many hundreds of years later tells us that the Bible isn't a "normal" book. It is, in fact, the inspired word of God. It is God's love letter to and instruction manual for His kids. It is the story of God creating an amazing world and paradise for mankind, only to have them mess it up. This required a Mess-iah, so God came to earth, became a man, lived a perfect sinless life, and died on the cross for the sins of all humanity, so once again God could have relationship with people.

Jesus lived a normal human life. His mother was a stay-at-home mom and his stepdad, Joseph, worked as a carpenter. Jesus grew up in wisdom and stature, just like all boys do. The first sign that he was someone special was when he was twelve. His parents brought him to Jerusalem for the annual sacrifice for sin. They left with a familial caravan and three days later realized that Jesus wasn't with them. They frantically arrived back in Jerusalem and after searching for some time, found Jesus in the temple wowing the religious leaders with his knowledge and understanding of scripture. When his parents scolded him, Jesus told them that he had to be in his Father's house. Jesus was referring to Father God. (See Luke 2:46-47)

Although there are no records, tradition has it that Jesus would have received formal education in the Jewish Synagogue beginning at age 5. He would have studied the Torah (first 5 books of the Bible) and memorized large portions of scripture. However, because his family wasn't wealthy, there was a time when the schooling stopped, and he began apprenticing under his father to become a craftsman. Although his disciples called him rabbi, he wasn't recognized as such by the Jewish leaders of his time. Since Jesus said that he never said anything except what he heard his father say, we can say that he was made a rabbi by God, not man.

Around age 30, Jesus left his occupation and began his ministry time. He gathered twelve men who became his disciples. They walked and lived with him for about three years. He taught them through words and his actions, then sent them out into the world around them to preach the gospel (good news of salvation), make disciples, cast out demons, and heal the sick. The lives of those disciples were very difficult and most of them died for their faith in Jesus. However, the result of their work two thousand years ago has resulted in approximately 2.4 billion Christians worldwide.

Jesus was a man of purpose. He was born with the purpose of teaching and preparing disciples to continue his work after his death. He was also born to die as the sacrificial lamb for the sin of all mankind. He was fully God and fully man, which is something we will never understand this side of heaven. God loved us so much that He sent His only Son to die for our sins (John 3:16). Jesus loved us so much that He left the glories of heaven and community with the Father and Spirit, to be born a helpless baby, grow into a man, teach, and disciple for three years, and then die a horrific death for us. That's an amazing love story and we are the focus of that love.

Although Jesus was sentenced to death by the Jewish religious leaders and the crucifixion carried out by the Romans, it was all part of God's plan to redeem mankind. Let's move into the next chapter and learn more about this plan.

CHAPTER THREE

THE GIFT OF GRACE

As I said in the second chapter, Jesus' sacrifice and shedding of blood on the cross of Calvary was enough to atone (make legal payment) for the sin of all mankind. No one is left out. That is called grace. Grace can be described as an unmerited act of mercy. It is a gift offered to humanity by God that eliminates our sin and allows us to have a right relationship (righteousness) with God. For those who have not yet received that gift, God is standing there with a big, beautiful gold wrapped box offering it to all who will receive. Now, you can look at that box and think it's big and beautiful and you want it, but if you don't actually reach out and receive it, you don't get the benefit of the gift.

The Bible (God's instruction manual for mankind)

clearly tells us that all have sinned and fallen short of the glory of God (Romans 3:23). It also tells us that the wages (payment) for sin is death, but the gift (grace) of God is eternal life in Christ Jesus our Lord (Romans 6:23). We are all born with sin and deserve the punishment for sin, which is an eternity of torture, away from God's love, in hell. But God demonstrated His own love for all of us in this way: While we were still sinners, Jesus died for us (in our place).

We were like prisoners on death row, awaiting execution, when a man comes in and takes our place. He is executed in our place, and we go free. That's the gift of grace that God offers. But, we also have a part to play. God gave us all free will, so we must choose to receive the gift of grace. "If you declare with your mouth, 'Jesus is Lord,' and believe in your heart that God raised him from the dead, you will be saved." (Romans 10:9) Our part is to believe in Jesus as our only Savior and to declare out loud (profess) that Jesus is our personal Savior and Lord. If you do that, you will be saved.

So, Jesus died for the sins of all humanity. Yes, for all those in the past, present and future. But there is a catch. It's a gift offered, but we must receive and embrace it. We don't have to work for it. It's a gift. All we must do is receive it. He offers this gift because He loves and wants a relationship with us.

That's a little mind blowing for me. I grew up thinking that God was some distant entity who was mad at, or at least disappointed in, me. Every time I did something wrong, He caused something bad to happen. Of course, I later learned that none of that was true. He is, in fact, a loving Father who wants the best for me. Out of that love, He does guide and disciplines me (and all of His kids) at times, so I don't get off the path and make a mess of my life. I wish I could say I stayed on the path, but I did veer off a few times. Fortunately, God guided me back to the path.

So, although Jesus died for the sins of all people, we must complete our part in the transaction. That is to receive the gift, and we do that by confessing that we are a sinner (born that way) in need of a Savior. Then we recognize and receive Jesus as that Savior. Followed by a commitment to live our life committed to God and day-by-day to become more like Jesus in how we sound, act, and react.

When we accept that amazing gift of grace and begin the process of becoming more like Jesus, our life will change. We will produce spiritual fruit, which we will examine further in chapter six.

CHAPTER FOUR

GOD AND SATAN

Since salvation is centered around God and many people don't believe in God, let's examine the proof that there is a God and more about who He is. As I previously mentioned in chapter one, God created the earth and mankind. He created man/Adam from the dirt and then breathed life into him. He created woman/Eve from the rib of Adam. They were created different and yet both are important to God's plan for ruling the earth and spreading His Kingdom.

God is Omnipresent

So, who is God? God is a spiritual being who has no beginning or end. God is omnipresent, which means that He is everywhere and in everything. In the Bible book of Genesis, it says that God spoke everything into existence, which means that everything physical started in the spiritual realm as God's voice. Hebrews 11:3 NKJV says, "By faith we understand that the worlds were framed by the word of God, so that the things which are seen were not made of things which are visible." If they weren't made from things visible, that means they were made from something invisible.

When I was a child, I knew that God was real. Not because someone told me, but rather because I could see God in the flowers, animals, people, and the sky. My grandmother had a cabin in the mountains of Colorado. There were many fields of wildflowers, and they were all different shapes and colors. It just seemed to me that God was an artist and had created each of those flowers to make this world more beautiful. I also saw all the animals and they were all so different. I knew that God had created them that way. Then there were people, who also are so amazingly different. I've never found anyone who looked exactly like me. God made us all unique. Finally, the sky. I was really into astronomy and loved studying the universe. My dad took me to an observatory, so I could look at planets and stars. I read about how big and precise the universe is. NASA can send an unmanned craft into space and know that it won't hit anything. None of that happens by accident. It all requires a Creator. It requires God. God is omnipresent – He is everywhere and in everything.

God is Omniscient

God is omniscient, which means He knows everything. You may think you are hiding your thoughts from God or getting away with sin but think again. He knows everything and sees everything. Unlike us, God doesn't operate in time. He sees and experiences everything all at the same time. He has seen the beginning and the end and everything in between. A pastor once explained it this way: We see like the person sitting in a car at a train crossing. The bars are down, and the train is going by slowly. It's a long one, so you are going to be there a while, watching each car go by. On the other hand, God sees the entire train at the same time. Every car simultaneously. It's a simple concept, but I think you get the idea.

Because God sees everything in the same moment, He can give people glimpses into the future. God did this through what the Bible calls a prophet and the glimpse into the future is called prophecy. According to J Barton Payne's *Encyclopedia of Biblical Prophecy*, there are 1239 prophecies in the Old Testament and 578 prophecies in the New Testament, for a total of 1817. Over half of those have been documented as fulfilled. The balance of the prophecies refers to the end of times, which are in the future. Because of the accuracy of those fulfilled, we can believe that God inspired the writing of the Bible, so we can have confidence that the rest of them will be fulfilled. Do you want to know what's going to happen in the future? Read the Bible.

Because God is omniscient, everything He does has intelligent purpose. He didn't just randomly create mankind; He created us with a purpose – to populate and rule the earth. We've done a banner job populating the earth, but it's our ruling that has caused all the issues we face in our world today.

God's omniscience is based on His authority. After all, He is the Creator of everything and the supreme judge of all things. This means that there is nothing that trumps God's word about what is true and what is false, or what is good and what is evil. People have spent thousands of years trying to be God, but it has always resulted in disaster. God is God and we are not.

God is Omnipotent

This means that God is all powerful. He is the most powerful being in the universe because He created everything in it. When scientists talk about a big bang that created the universe, they are really talking about the power of God's voice speaking it into existence. The Bible predicts that there will come a time when the resurrected Jesus returns to the earth in His God power. He will speak to the rebellious armies of the world that have come against Him, and they will all die. That's true power. No other being has that kind of power.

Because of this reference to being all powerful, people often say that God can do anything, but there are things that God can't do. He is a holy God, so

He can't lie. Nor can He do anything immoral or evil. He also can do nothing that would contradict something He has already said in His Word, the Bible.

God used His power to create this world, make mankind, and then save us by using His power to come to earth as a human child. It was that power that raised Jesus from the dead. Jesus used that same power to raise Lazarus from the dead. He also gives that power to all who are saved, through the Holy Spirit living in each person who has received Jesus as their Savior.

When the world was too big a mess and the thoughts of man where just evil all the time (kind of sounds like the world we live in today), God used His power to flood the earth. But, because He loved mankind, He saved Noah (the only righteous man) and his family and enabled them to re-populate the earth. There were also times when He used his power to open the earth and swallow rebellious people. God's power is endless and there is no one who can come against Him.

God is Love

We all have heard about and experienced love, but only God is love (1 John 4:8). This doesn't mean He acts out of love, rather that He is actually love. This means that everything He does is out of love. For example, when Adam and Eve rebelled against God by eating the forbidden fruit, it was out of love that He removed them of the Garden of Eden. The tree of life was also in Eden and God knew that if He allowed His kids to stay in the Garden, they would suffer with guilt and shame for all eternity. So, through love, God moved them into the world, where they would eventually die.

It was out of love that God let a whale swallow rebellious Jonah and kept him sheltered in the whale for three days. It was out of love that God called Moses to lead the Israelites out of Egyptian slavery. It was out of love that God sent His Son to be born a human child, live a normal human life, and then die a horrible death for the sins of mankind. It was out of love that the Son left the glories of heaven, set aside His godly attributes, and confined Himself to a human womb. It was out of love for us that Jesus endured the pain of the cross.

The truth is that without God, we can't love. We can be infatuated and lustful, but we cannot love. Love is not an emotion; it's the obedient act of allowing God to love through us. Infatuation and lust don't last, but God's love does.

Because God is love, He is a very personal being. He truly loves all of us. No matter what we do, He still loves us. He may discipline us to get us back on the right path, but He does it all through love because that's what He is. God loves the worst of sinners.

Saul was one of those. He was a Jewish religious leader who was having Christians killed and imprisoned. However, one moment in God's love changed Saul forever and he became Paul, the apostle and writer of a large part of the Bible's New Testament.

God is Just

Many people ask how a loving God could send people to hell. That's a false view of God, as He doesn't send anyone to hell. As was discussed earlier, we make the choice of our eternal destination – heaven or hell. It was man who messed everything up by being rebellious. God said that Adam and Eve could eat from every tree in Eden, except the tree of the knowledge of good and evil. God gave them free will but didn't want them to have to experience evil. All they knew was God's perfect good, until they rebelled and ate from that tree. Through that same free will, mankind has been rebelling ever since. So, because God is a just God, there must be punishment for rebellion.

Let's take a break from that thought and use something we are more familiar with. In our court system, if a judge allowed convicted murderers to go free, he would be an unjust judge, and the judicial system would fall apart. It's the same in God's court, because He is a just judge, He can't allow sin to go unpunished. The good news, as we discussed earlier, is that Jesus took that punishment for our sin, so all we must do is accept that gift of grace.

Those who do accept Jesus as their Savior will go to heaven and those who don't make the choice to spend eternity in hell. I'll share more about heaven and hell in the next chapter.

God in Three Persons

God represents Himself to mankind in three persons. We see the three represented when Jesus spoke in Matthew 28:19 saying to his disciples, "Go therefore and make disciples of all nations, baptizing them in the name of the Father and the Son and the Holy Spirit." There we have it, the three persons of God – Father, Son, and Holy Spirit. The Son is also known as Jesus, the person of God who was born a human child and later died on the cross for the sins of all mankind. Jesus told people that if they had seen him, they had seen the Father. He didn't mean his physical body, as Father God doesn't have a physical body, but rather his spiritual nature, because God is Spirit and He is everywhere.

Father God has been and is always on the throne in heaven, but through His Spirit, the Holy Spirit, He is also all throughout the earth. So, the Holy Spirit is not an "it" or a "power," He is one of the persons of God. Not only is He all throughout the earth, but He is also in every person who receives Jesus as their Savior. In the Bible, the Holy Spirit is also referred to as the Spirit of Jesus and the Spirit of Truth. He is also called the Helper, Comforter, Counselor, Advocate, Guide, Intercessor, Revealer, Spirit of Life, Teacher, Witness, and the one who convicts humanity of their sins. The Holy Spirit is the person of God that connects us with and points us to the Father and Jesus.

Jesus was and is God in flesh. In John 1, it refers to Jesus as the Word and says that in the beginning, the Word was with God and the Word was God, and that everything was created by the Word. It also says that the Word became flesh and dwelled among mankind. The Word is the person of God who became the man Jesus. Jesus was the only person ever to be fully God and fully man. Don't even try to figure that one out. It's beyond our human brain power. Jesus was God in flesh. He also said that he was the image of the invisible God (Colossians 1:15), so by studying what Jesus said, what he did, how he acted and reacted, we can gain a better understanding of the Father.

Satan is Not Equal to God

God is perfect and always good. On the flip side is Satan or the devil. Let's take a moment to examine him. First, he is not equal to God, as many people think. Second, Satan is not everywhere at the same time, all powerful, and all-knowing like God. Actually, Satan was an angel, named Lucifer, created by God. It appears that he was one of the archangels like Michael and Gabriel. They would be his equal, not God. So, how did Lucifer become Satan?

Lucifer had spent all eternity in the presence of

God, experiencing the ongoing worship. He was the classic guy who wanted the boss's job. So, he gets a bunch of his co-workers together to rebel against the boss. It was pride that caused Lucifer to lead one third of the angels in rebellion against God. They were defeated by Michael and the other two thirds of the angels and cast out of heaven. Satan and these fallen angels are what we know of as demons. They hate God and God's children, so their sole function is to steal, kill, and destroy the lives of men and women. They do this by manipulating people with lies. Satan did it in the Garden of Eden and he and his minions continue to do it today.

I don't see it as much anymore, but there used to be cartoons where the person would have a devil on one shoulder and an angel on the other. They battled to get the person to do bad or good. There is some truth to that. Every day is a battle of making the right decisions. The first right decision, that the devil doesn't want you to make, is to accept Jesus as your Savior and begin living your life for Him.

A few more things about the devil. He is not a guy in a red suit with a spikey tail and pitchfork. It's comical and so I imagine the devil loves that because people don't take him seriously. That said, the devil is real. His greatest lie has been convincing people that he doesn't exist. He is real and he wants to destroy your life, but he has no control over you, and he can't make you do things. He can only whisper lies into your thoughts. If you accept, dwell and act on those lies, then the devil wins. If you, as the Bible says, take those thoughts captive and reject them, then God wins and so do you. Here's the key to knowing if it's God or Satan. God's thoughts will always be good, uplifting, and pure. Satan's thoughts will be evil, impure, and will be attractive to your selfish flesh nature rather than your spirit.

Even though the devil is not omnipresent (everywhere at one time), he is cunning, organized, strategic, and has an army of fallen angels at his beck and call. They all have one goal, to destroy the lives of those who believe in Jesus. The good news is that Lucifer (now known as Satan or the devil) was only able to sway one third of the angels in his rebellion. That means there are two thirds of the angels still submitted to serving God. If you have received Jesus as your Savior, then those angels are fighting for you in the spirit realm (which is another dimension all around us).

Satan's only real weapon is lies. Jesus referred to him as the father of lies and that everything that comes out of his mouth is a lie. At the beginning of the book, we saw how he lied to Eve and Adam to deceive them into disobeying God. Satan continues to do the same today. One thing is for sure, he isn't creative, but since his basic lies are still working, he doesn't need to be. The good news is that his consistency makes him predictable and allows us to be prepared by studying God's Word (the Bible) and seeking God in prayer.

Salvation is really about a choice – to follow God or follow the devil. In the next chapter, you will learn how this choice impacts your eternal destination.

Eternity is a very, very, very long time, so I hope to help you make the right decision.

CHAPTER FIVE

HELL AND HEAVEN

Hell

As I mentioned previously, I'm constantly hearing people ask why a loving God would send people to hell. Well, the truth is, He doesn't. We are the ones who make that choice. The good news is that God gave us a way out and that's what we're going to talk about in this chapter. Again, it's my hope that I can help you make the right choice for your eternal destination and that's heaven. But first, let's talk about the alternate location – hell.

Contrary to what a lot of people are teaching and thinking, hell is a very real place. It is a place of eternal torture in fire. Imagine if your skin were constantly burned by fire 24/7 and you could never die. That's hell. Imagine also, total darkness with no contact with any other person for the rest of eternity. Also, imagine that while your skin is burned by fire, your insides are slowly and painfully eaten by worms, but you can never die. Lastly, imagine that there is no presence of God's love. Even if you don't believe in Him, He loves you. His love for you and all of humanity is always present. Although we don't think about it and take His love for granted, we have never been without God's love. But, in hell, His love will be absent. Finally, imagine that you can never die or leave. There is no way out. Can you imagine the hopelessness?

How do we know that hell is real? Because the Bible talks about it. Jesus talked about it. How do we know the Bible is right? Because the Bible is inspired by God. How do we know that? Because the Bible is the only prophetic document ever written with 100% accuracy. I've never personally counted the number of prophecies, but the number seems to be between 1800 and 2500. Noted biblical scholar, Dr. John F. Walvoord covers 1000 key prophecies, backed with solid scriptural evidence, in his amazing book, *Every Prophecy of the Bible*.

Biblical prophecies include natural disasters, times of economic uncertainty, rise and fall of powerful empires, political uprisings, destruction of key buildings, the miraculous birth of Jesus the Messiah, detailed accounts of how Jesus would die, the rise of the antichrist leader, the seven-year tribulation, and the return of Jesus to rule the world. Well over half of all biblical prophecies have been documented as fulfilled. Show me another book or person who has that type of accuracy. Only God, who knows all, could have done that.

So, given the extreme accuracy of the Bible, we can be assured that hell is real. But the truth is, it wasn't created for mankind. Rather, it was created for Lucifer (now Satan or the devil) and the angels that followed him in rebellion against God. The Bible also refers to hell as the lake of fire and says that in the end, Satan will be thrown into the lake of fire to be tortured for all eternity. He will be joined by all the rebellious angels and unfortunately, many rebellious people. Even though hell was not created for mankind, when Adam and Eve chose to be disobedient to God, they destined all of mankind to spend eternity in hell. As I talked about earlier in the book, every human born from that point on, was born with a sinful nature. We are all sinners and have fallen short of the glory of God. No matter how good we think we are, we all deserve eternity in hell. But God made a way out. Jesus is the way. Recognize that Jesus sacrificed himself on the cross for your sins and receive him as your Savior, and you punch your eternal ticket to heaven instead of hell. With that said, let's shift gears and talk about heaven.

Heaven

Heaven also is real. The Bible tells us so. In fact, it's where God lives. It is interesting that the Bible talks about three heavens. The first is the heaven we see – our atmosphere and space with the sun, planets, moons, and distant solar systems or what we call the universe. That is the first heaven, and it was created by God. Our planet, earth, is part of that heaven. It's physical. We can see and touch and smell it.

The second heaven is not physical. It is a spiritual realm where angels and fallen angels or demons live. They are all spiritual beings living in what we would think of as another dimension that occupies the same space as earth. We can't see them, but they are there. As we read in the Bible, there have been and continue to be times when angels show up as humans to interact with us. The most famous of these is when the angel Gabriel showed himself to a teenage girl named Mary and told her she would be pregnant by the Holy Spirit and would give birth to the Savior of the world, Jesus. It is rare for angels to show themselves in human form, but they are still there.

The third heaven is where the throne room of God is, along with special angels who are always around the throne. It's also where Jesus is seated at the right hand of the Father. Plus, it's the future home of all those who make the choice to receive Jesus as their Savior.

I often hear someone ask, why doesn't everyone go to heaven? Some people even believe that. Well, first if that were true, then heaven would look exactly like earth does right now. It would be full of violence, rape, child molestation, pornography, sex-trafficking, wars, poverty, famine, and so forth. Is that a place you would want to live in for all eternity? I surely don't!

The key here is that, as was discussed earlier, God is a just God, or you might say a just judge. You wouldn't expect a just judge to let convicted murderers go, would you? No, you would expect that there was punishment through separation – either prison or death. Well, it's the same with God as the judge. That said, unlike the world system, we have an advocate named Jesus who doesn't just represent us in the court of heaven, He took the punishment we deserved. You don't ever hear of an innocent person taking the place of a guilty person and voluntarily receiving their punishment and yet that is exactly what Jesus did for you and me. The best news is that it's called salvation and it's available to every person. No matter how good or bad we have been, our loving heavenly Father is waiting with open arms to receive us.

There will come a day when we will all pass away. Our physical bodies will go into the ground or be cremated, but our spirits will go on living forever either in heaven or in hell. Unlike this world, there is no middle ground and it's our choice. It's your choice.

CHAPTER SIX

THE PROOF IS IN THE FRUIT

Earlier in the book, we examined why we need salvation and how that happens, but how can we be assured that we are secure in that salvation. Well, according to the Bible, the proof is in the fruit. Scripture teaches us that we are like trees. If a fruit tree is properly rooted and has water, it will naturally grow fruit – oranges, apples, lemons, and so on. It's the same with us. If we are properly rooted in Jesus and receiving His living water, then we will supernaturally produce spiritual fruit.

Before we talk about that type of fruit, let's examine the fruit that we produce if we are connected to the world and its ways. The Bible, in Galatians 5:19-21, tells us that the fruit of the flesh are obvious: sexual immorality, impurity and debauchery; idolatry and witchcraft; hatred, discord, jealousy, fits of rage, selfish ambition, dissensions, factions, and envy; drunkenness, orgies, and the like. As I look back over my life, before I encountered Jesus and received Him as my Savior, I resembled that list. Perhaps you did or do now. This is naturally what happens if we are rooted in the world.

The Bible tells us not to be conformed to the ways of the world, rather to be transformed by the renewing of our mind. Only the Bible can do that. Only a constant inflow of scripture can transform a worldly mind. I tried many of the worldly ways – self-help, meditation, hypnosis, even religion, but nothing changed. Then I met Jesus and turned my life over to Him and everything changed. Not instantly, it took some time, as God pruned the worldly stuff out of my life, so that I could produce spiritual fruit. He will lovingly do the same for you.

So, how does the Bible describe that spiritual fruit? Galatians 5:22-23 says: love, joy, peace, patience, kindness, goodness, faithfulness, gentleness, and self-control. Doesn't that sound a whole lot better than that first list? Who wouldn't want that kind of change? Yet many fight it because they have to give up things. Well, yes, but these are bad things that bring on destruction and death. The choice was hard for me at first, but now it's easy and I can't imagine anyone choosing the fruit of the world over the fruit that comes from rooting ourselves in Jesus.

My fruit test is always when I'm under pressure. That's the time when anger tries to pop up its ugly head again or where one of those worldly words wants to fly out of my mouth. Under pressure, your fruit will get squeezed, and in those moments, what will come out of you?

So, much like in the previous chapter, you have a choice of which type of fruit you will produce. If you choose Jesus and a future in heaven, and stay rooted in Him, you will produce that wonderful heavenly fruit. Otherwise, you will produce some stinking ugly fruit and spend eternity in hell. The choice is always yours.

God is rooting for you and so am I. Choose Jesus. If you are ready to make that choice, it's simple, just pray this prayer: *Father God, I admit that I am a sinner in need of a Savior. I receive Jesus as my personal Savior. Holy Spirit come and fill me. Teach me. Guide me. Help me. Father, I thank you for loving me so much and adopting me into your family. I commit to living the rest of my life for you.*

If you prayed that prayer from your heart and really meant it, then you are SAVED. Congratulations! You now have a ticket to heaven. That said, your journey has just begun. The point is not getting the ticket to heaven, it's living this life the way God intended. He had you born on this earth at this specific time in history for a purpose. There are no accidents living on the earth. We are all part of His grand plan to make the earth look like heaven. So, what do you do next? I'll cover that in the next chapter.

CHAPTER SEVEN

WHAT'S NEXT

Once again, congratulations on choosing Jesus and heaven! Excellent choice. One day you will pass from this world to the next and stand face-to-face with the one who died for you and made all of this possible. He will welcome you into heaven and then there will be a moment when all your earthly actions and words will be judged. Not for salvation, because that was settled when you prayed, but rather, it is for rewards.

1 Corinthians 3:11-15 teaches us, "For no one can lay any foundation other than the one already laid, which is Jesus Christ. [12] If anyone builds on this foundation using gold, silver, costly stones, wood, hay, or straw, [13] their work will be shown for what it is, because the Day will bring it to light. It will be

revealed with fire, and the fire will test the quality of each person's work. [14] If what has been built survives, the builder will receive a reward. [15] If it is burned up, the builder will suffer loss but yet will be saved—even though only as one escaping through the flames."

In simpler words, all the worldly things you did like jobs, businesses, investing, traveling and the material things you bought for your own pleasure will burn in the Fire of God as wood, hay, and straw. Whereas the things you do for God and spreading His Kingdom throughout the earth will turn into gold, silver, and precious stones. I believe that Jesus will use these materials to create crowns, but the crowns are not for us, they are to present back to Jesus as an offering of our love.

All that said, you want to spend the rest of the time you have here on earth doing things that will survive the Fire. Here are a few of those:

1. **Love God** – In Luke 10:27, Jesus taught those following him, "Love the Lord your God with all your heart and with all your soul and with all your strength and with all your mind' and 'Love your neighbor as yourself.'" That is a lot of "all's." An easier way to put that would be to love God with everything you have. He should be your number one love, above everything and everyone this earth offers. As with any love affair, you must invest time to get to know

God. You will learn more about that in the following points. As you develop a true love for God, you will also begin loving people more. Yes, even those who are seemingly unlovable and those who come against you. The good news is that it won't be you; it will be God loving through you.

2. **Find a Good Bible Teaching and Holy Spirit Filled Church** – One of the keys to your growth in loving God and loving other people is to be part of a good church. If you have friends who attend church, ask them where they go. If not, then jump on the internet and do a search for "Holy Spirit filled churches near me." Generally, you can go on the church web site and watch services and messages, look at what they believe, see pictures of people, and review what ministries they offer, such as small groups, men's or women's ministry, children's, or youth (if you have children). If you have a family, you want to make sure they are all walking with you on this journey. When you find one that looks good, go visit. The right church will feel like home.

3. **Study God's Word** – Remember early in this book, I mentioned that Jesus is referred to as "the Word" in the gospel of John. The

Word was the one who spoke everything into existence. The Bible is also referred to as God's Word, so when you read and study the scriptures, you are actually hearing from Jesus. Yes, Jesus is speaking from Genesis to Revelation. The really amazing thing about the Bible is that it's not like other books. It is inspired by God and is His living Word. It will speak to you. Not in an audible voice, but in your mind. You can also ask questions and have conversations with God (more on that in the next point). So, if you don't have a Bible, buy one. I recommend getting an NIV or NLT Life Application Bible. They are a little more expensive, but worth it, as you get commentary notes that will help you understand the scriptures better. I would also recommend that you ask at your church about Bible studies and find some other people you can study the scriptures with. If you can't afford to buy a Bible, ask someone at your church and I'm sure they will find a Bible for you.

4. **Prayer** – Prayer is not saying the same thing over and over or bringing your list of wants to a cosmic Santa Claus. Rather, it is talking with God. Now, He's probably not going to talk with you in an audible voice, but you will still hear His voice in your thoughts. Since you are now His child, He loves hearing about your life (even though He

knows everything). He wants to hear about the good, bad, and the ugly. Bring your success and struggles to Him. You can talk with Him all throughout your day – while you are showering, dressing, eating, driving, exercising, working, and so on. He loves being part of your day. Now, it's also okay for you to bring your needs to Him. He loves to help His kids (and you are now one of them). Just know that He always hears and answers our prayers, but not always in the timing or the way we would like or expect. So, be patient with the answers.

There are many other disciplines that are important to your growth in relationship with God. Things like worship, serving, tithing, and giving, fasting, journaling, and evangelizing. All of these will come in time. Right now, focus on the first four and you will be on your way to an excellent journey with the Lord.

AUTHOR'S NOTE

NOTE: If you prayed the prayer to receive Jesus for the first time, please let me know by emailing me at rod@rodnichols.com. I would love to hear the good news, answer any questions you have, and be praying for you. I hope to hear from you.

NOTE 2: When someone gets saved, they are typically very excited about it and want to tell other people. That's a good thing and Jesus told us to do that. However, you're probably not going to have the right words to speak, so use this book to introduce people to salvation. Order extra copies and say something like this: *I just read this great book. I'd love to loan it to you, if you will read it."* If they say yes, then arrange a day to get it back and on that day, say: *Did you read the book? So, what do you think?* If they prayed the prayer, celebrate with them and make sure you help them get connected with a church and start studying the Bible. If they didn't pray the prayer, but you get something positive back, share your story of how you got saved and then invite them to receive Christ. If it's still a no, that's okay. You've planted seeds. Start praying for them to get saved. God will do a good work.

Many Blessings to you,

Rod

ABOUT THE AUTHOR

Rod Nichols was called by God out of a successful business career to launch ministries, plant churches, write books, and equip the body of Christ. He serves as the Executive and Teaching Pastor at AZ Vineyard Church in Goodyear, Arizona. Rod is also the founder of the True Disciple Academy, an online Bible school, which you find at TrueDiscipleAcademy.com. He has published twelve books, including *True Disciple, God's Financial Plan,* and *Where Did All the People Go?*

OTHER BOOKS BY ROD NICHOLS

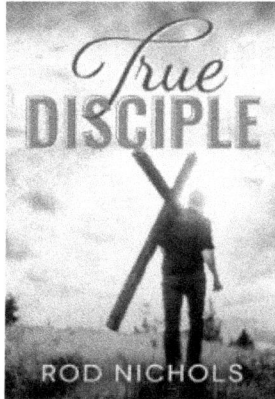

Throughout the Bible we find ordinary, fallible people just like us. These ordinary people did extraordinary things. Then along came Jesus. He said that his followers would do even greater things than he did. A mind-blowing promise! Yet, most believers haven't experienced the miracles we see in God's Word. What is the difference between the people in the Bible and those sitting in any of our churches?

The answer to that question is found in Rod Nichols' book, *True Disciple*. Rod believes the Lord instructed him to write his true disciple story. He was (and still is) one of those ordinary, fallible people that God taught to be a true disciple of Jesus Christ. Rod is real and transparent about his struggles, doubts, fears, questions, and failures. He shares some amazing adventures and what he learned along the way. With God's help, these lessons could transform any ordinary person into a mountain moving true disciple.

In *True Disciple*, Nichols hopes to motivate the church to love God with all they have and to love people as Jesus loved us; to get out from those comfy seats and secure walls and go do what Jesus commanded - preach the gospel to the world, make disciples, heal, deliver, and help those in need. Are you ready for the adventure of a lifetime? Would you like to have God use you to change the world around you? True Disciple will prepare you for an amazing journey!

Order on Amazon.

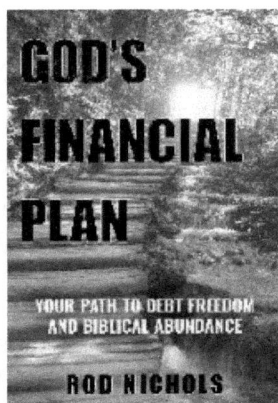

GOD'S FINANCIAL PLAN

YOUR PATH TO DEBT FREEDOM
AND BIBLICAL ABUNDANCE

ROD NICHOLS

Are you experiencing debt and financial struggles? Does it feel hopeless at times? Well, it's not, because God has a financial plan for you. All you have to do is learn about and implement the plan in your life. That's what the author, Rod Nichols, did. He and his wife were $120,000 in debt, feeling lost and hopeless. Yet, after entering into God's financial plan, they were debt free in just five years and have remained so to this day.

God did not create you to be poor and to struggle financially. He created you to live the abundant life that Jesus died for. He created you to help finance the growth of the His Kingdom here on earth. He created you to prosper in every part of your life, which includes finances.

In this book, Rod Nichols shares the scripture-based plan that God has for the financial lives of His children. He also shares practical tips that God gave him for getting out of debt and increasing your income. These are proven concepts that have worked for Rod and many others, and they will work for you.

It's time for you to get out of debt and begin enjoying biblical abundance.

Order on Amazon.

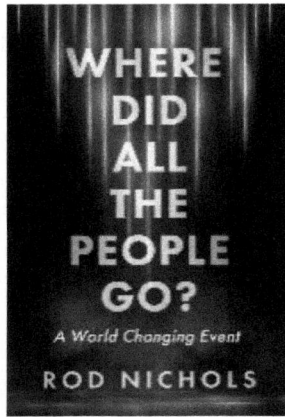

WHERE DID ALL THE PEOPLE GO?

A World Changing Event

ROD NICHOLS

Depending on when you are reading this book, either millions, possibly billions of people have disappeared or will disappear soon. The world is or will be in total chaos as it enters the worst time in world history.

If this disappearance has not happened yet, then this book will unveil the future and give you instructions on what to do before people disappear. It's also a great book to share with family and friends, so they too can make the right decision, before it's too late.

If people have already disappeared, then this book will give you a clear and accurate picture of what will happen in the years to come. Read and study the book carefully, as you will have a second chance to make the right decision, but it will come at a cost.

For those who are living before the mass disappearance, leave copies of this book in your home, office, and vehicles, so that those who are left behind can read and understand what has happened and what is to come.

Order on Amazon